W9-BHR-674

37653010395005
McMath JUV NonFiction
JUV
362.5 WOLF
Homeless

CENTRAL ARKANSAS LIBRARY SYSTEM
SIDNEY S. McMATH BRANCH LIBRARY
LITTLE ROCK, ARKANSAS

HOMELESS

Written and photographed by BERNARD WOLF

ORCHARD BOOKS • New York

Author's Note

Since 1893, the Henry Street Settlement has successfully proven—not only to New York City but also to the nation—what enlightened philanthropy can achieve. A half century ago, it established the first mental health clinic in the United States. Its ever-expanding array of programs ranges from assistance to new immigrants to social services and counseling for the disadvantaged and adult education and training in the creative arts. In 1972, the Urban Family Center became one of the United States' first transitional housing projects for the homeless and has since become a model for others to emulate. Its motto is "Families may be homeless but not helpless."

Acknowledgments

For their generous support and assistance in the preparation of this book, I wish to thank the following persons: Daniel Kronenfeld, executive director, Henry Street Settlement, New York City; Dea Spencer, associate director, Henry Street Settlement Urban Family Center; Hector Perez and Jerry Purnell, social workers, and Alberto Gonzalez, educational guidance counselor, Henry Street Settlement Urban Family Center; Ann Scarola and Rosalie Lucchese, third- and fourth-grade teachers, P.S. 97, New York City. Special thanks to Mikey's mother, Sharon, for her courage, patience, and understanding; to my editors, Neal Porter and Maggie Herold; and to my designer, Sallie Baldwin.

Copyright © 1995 by Bernard Wolf

All rights reserved. No part of this book may be reproduced or transmitted in any form or by any means, electronic or mechanical, including photocopying, recording, or by any information storage or retrieval system, without permission in writing from the Publisher.

ORCHARD BOOKS
95 Madison Avenue, New York, NY 10016

Manufactured in Singapore. Printed and bound by Toppan Printing Company, Inc.
Book design by The Antler & Baldwin Design Group

10 9 8 7 6 5 4 3 2 1

The text of this book is set in 16 point ITC Berkeley Old Style Book. All of the pictures were made with Nikon equipment. I used an 8008S body. My lenses were a 24mm AF F2.8, a 35mm AF F2, and a 60mm AF F2.8 micro-Nikkor. An SB25 speed light was used for fill flash. My film was Fujichrome 100.

Library of Congress Cataloging-in-Publication Data

Wolf, Bernard, date.
 Homeless/written and photographed by Bernard Wolf.
   p.   cm.
   ISBN 0-531-06886-2.–ISBN 0-531-08736-0 (lib. bdg.)
    1. Homeless children—New York (N.Y.)—Juvenile literature. 2. Henry Street Settlement (New York, N.Y.)—Juvenile Literature.
3. Shelters for the homeless—New York (N.Y.)—Juvenile literature. [1. Homeless persons. 2. Poor—New York (N.Y.) 3. Family
life—New York (N. Y.)] I. Title. HV4506.N6W64 1995   362.5´09747´1–dc20   94-27293

CENTRAL ARKANSAS LIBRARY SYSTEM
SIDNEY S. McMATH BRANCH LIBRARY
LITTLE ROCK, ARKANSAS

This book is for Mikey
and for the millions of children of poverty
of America.

My name is Mikey and I'm eight years old. The last two nights were the worst of my life. I stayed with my family in an emergency shelter for the homeless. It was a huge room filled with other homeless people, some of them drunks and drug addicts. If we wanted to sleep, we had to stretch out on hard plastic chairs. But we hardly slept at all because we were afraid somebody might steal our extra clothes. Now they've sent us to another shelter called the Henry Street Settlement Urban Family Center. It's on the Lower East Side in New York City.

For two years, me, my little sisters and brother, my mother, and my stepfather have been moving from one place to another. We couldn't pay the rent for a good apartment, so finally my mom, Sharon, had to put us in the public shelter system for the homeless.

Today is almost the end of winter. Even though it's not too cold, we're all wearing lots of layers of clothes. My stepfather, Sergio, has to carry the rest of our stuff in two big plastic bags.

A man called Mr. Perez comes out to meet us. He shakes everybody's hand and says to call him Hector.

Then he takes us to a big room where we can talk. He'll be our caseworker. He seems like a nice guy, but I'm kind of nervous. I don't know what to expect in this place.

Hector tells my mom and Sergio that we'll get a rent-free apartment here, though it probably won't be for longer than nine months. Meanwhile, the center's staff will try to get us a permanent apartment. Hector asks my mom to sign an agreement that she will stick to the center's rules and understands that the apartment won't be permanent. Right now, Mom has no money. Hector gives her twenty-five dollars' worth of emergency food vouchers. Then he takes us out to our new place.

There's six apartment buildings in the center. Our apartment is on the fifth floor of one of these, but there's no elevator. It's a long climb up. I'm just wondering if we're going to another cold and dirty dump full of cockroaches. I hate them.

Hector unlocks the door and turns on the lights. I guess none of us were expecting anything like this. It's a small apartment and the furniture is nothing fancy, but it's warm and squeaky clean. There's even a crib for my baby sister, Laura. She's ten months old. After some of the places we've lived in, this looks pretty neat to me.

Destiny wants the top bunk. That's okay with me—I'm just glad we're here. Hector gives Mom a set of keys and wishes our family luck. He says if we have any problems, we should come to the office and he'll be there to help.

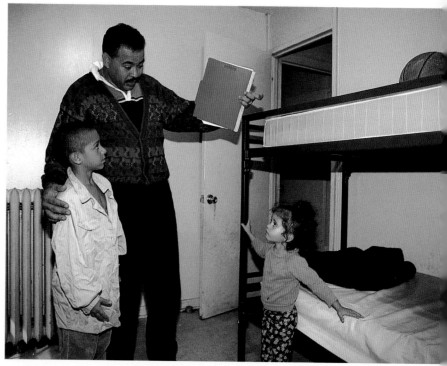

Hector shows Mom the kitchen and explains how the stove works. He shows her and Sergio their bedroom. They'll sleep there with my two-year-old brother, Sergio Jr. Then Hector shows me the room I'll be sharing with Destiny, my three-year-old sister. There's only space for a low chest of drawers and a double-decker bed.

Sergio starts unpacking, but Mom is really tired. All she wants to do is get out of her sweaty clothes, take a long shower with lots of hot water, and sleep under clean sheets for the first time in three days.

This Saturday morning, Mom will get and cash her public assistance check, which comes every two weeks. She leaves Destiny with a neighbor and her little girl. Then the rest of us all go to a nearby check-cashing office and wait in line. Mom's check will be for $284. Today is specially important because she'll also get her monthly allowance of food stamps, worth $367. Without those, she says, we'd be in *really* bad shape.

Sergio says he's going to look for a job. He'd like to be a policeman, but he can't without a high school diploma. That's going to take hard work.

When we finally reach the cashier's window, Mom shows her I.D. card. The teller gets her check. After she signs the back, he slides her money and food stamps through the window slot. Now we can go and do our big monthly shopping at the huge supermarket fifteen blocks away.

I enjoy shopping. We all love meat, but until today there's been no money to buy any. Mom tries to stock up on the cheapest kinds of meats and chicken. She needs to buy enough to last us for a month. Then we get some green peppers, onions, and garlic. She uses these to fix rice and beans. Meanwhile, Sergio picks up a bunch of cold cuts for sandwiches.

Now it's my turn. Mom asks me to choose some cereals for me and Destiny. I pick out a big box of Froot Loops.

Mom needs disposable diapers and baby food for Laura and Sergio Jr., paper towels, soap detergent, and toilet paper. Then she needs to get food to last us till next month—pasta, sauces, rice, beans, bread, snacks for us kids, fruit juices, and canned things—as well as gallons of milk and eggs and butter.

While Mom and Sergio are rushing around, I try to keep Sergio Jr. happy. He's just learning to talk a little. It's fun trying to teach him new words. By the time we line up at the checkout counter, we've got two big shopping carts piled high. Mom counts out her food stamps, but she has to pay cash for the things that aren't food. The bill comes to $278.39.

After unloading everything from a cab, Sergio runs upstairs to bring down a cart. Mom guards what we've bought on the sidewalk in front of our building. Sergio has to haul the loaded cart up five flights of stairs. On his third and last trip, we all go up.

Sergio cleans out our refrigerator. Mom needs to catch her breath. Tonight I know we're going to have a *really* good meal!

Two weeks after we got here, my mother put me in P.S. 97, right around the corner. It's the fifth school I've been in since we started moving around. I usually get up at 6:45 A.M. Then I go to the kitchen to fix breakfast for me and Destiny. We watch our favorite programs on TV while we eat our cereal. The TV means a lot to all of us. We can't afford to go to movies.

I've been going to P.S. 97 for about four months now. That's almost a record for me. I like my third-grade teacher, Miss Scarola, but I hate this school. I'm pretty small for my age. Some of the kids in my class are a lot bigger and tougher than me. One of them keeps punching me every chance he gets. I'm just hanging on till summer vacation—a couple of weeks more.

My teacher says I'm a bright student. She's right! She also says I have trouble concentrating. I guess she's right about that too.

The noise in the school cafeteria is real loud, but nobody minds. We get free lunch here every day. There are a lot of other homeless kids in this school. Some of them eat breakfast and dinner in school too. Sometimes I do when my mom's money is running out. Today we get a big chunk of pizza with chocolate milk and ice cream. I swap my pizza for another kid's milk and ice cream—not a bad trade!

After lunch, we go out to the school playground. My mom says that, because I'm so small, I try to act older than I am. Well, I do like to organize the games I play with other kids, but I always try to be friendly.

By the time my class is dismissed, it's been a pretty good day, only I've *still* got homework to do.

Mom has a new caseworker. His name is Jerry Purnell. He says he's applying for an apartment for us in the Mitchell-Lama program. Those are the best apartments homeless people can get. Mom is excited. She says that, more than anything else, she wants a permanent home for us in a good, safe neighborhood. Jerry warns her not to be too hopeful. He'll do his best, but there aren't many apartments big enough for families our size. There's no telling how long it could take. We've been living at the center for five months now. Mom knows a family's average stay is nine months. What happens if they can't find an apartment for us?

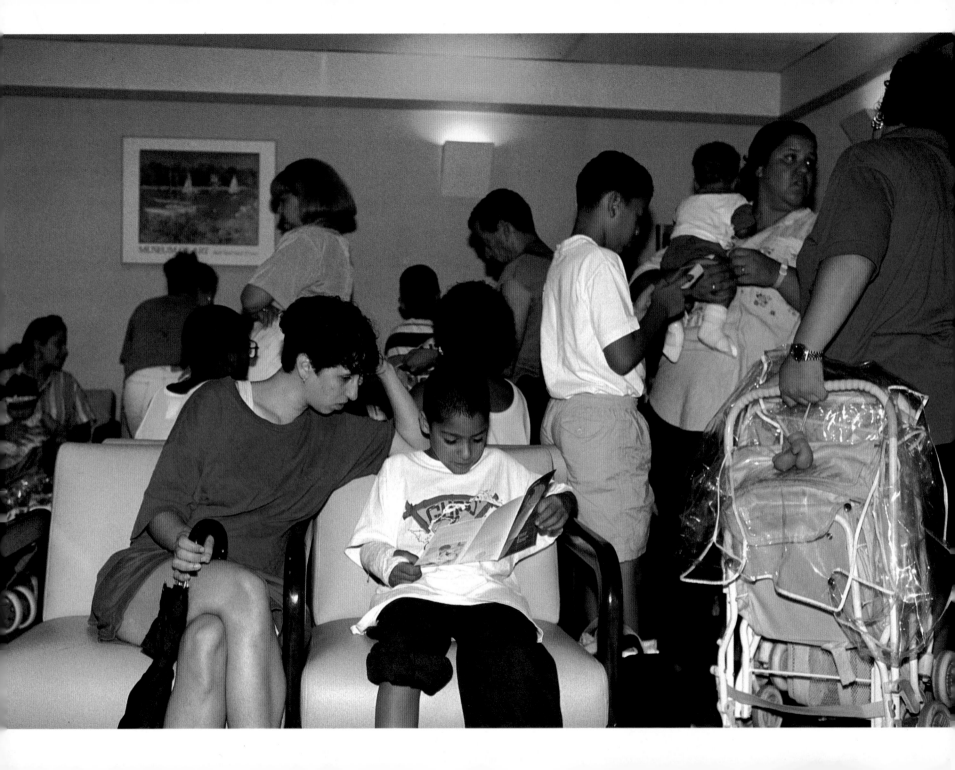

Well, my summer vacation has finally started—but not without a hitch. After school let out, I fell and broke my wrist, chasing a ball. Mom took me to the hospital. They took X rays and gave me a temporary cast and medicine. Now we're back again. It's only 8:30 A.M., but there's a mob of people waiting ahead of us in the clinic. An hour later, we get to register at the desk. Mom has Medicaid, so we don't have to pay for doctors and stuff.

I like to find out how things work. I grab a folder from a rack and read about broken arms and legs and how they are fixed.

At 10:30, we go in to see the doctor. He's put my X rays up on a lit panel. He asks if I can show him where the problem is. I point to a thin line on an X ray. The doctor says it's a hairline fracture of the wrist.

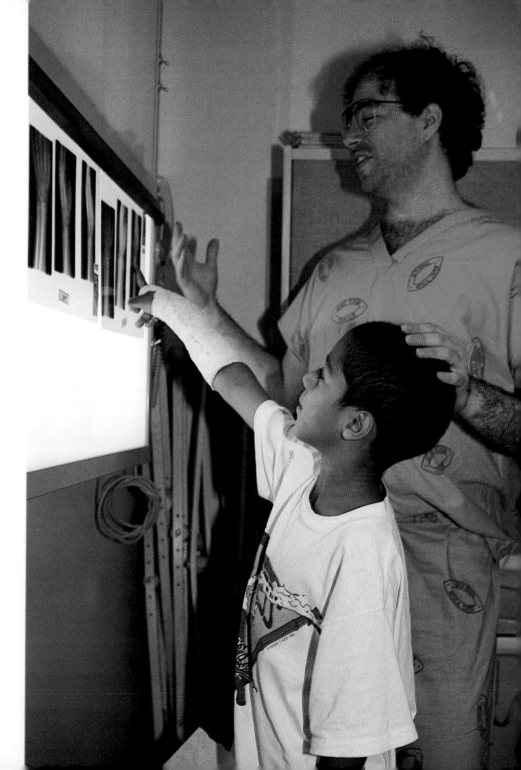

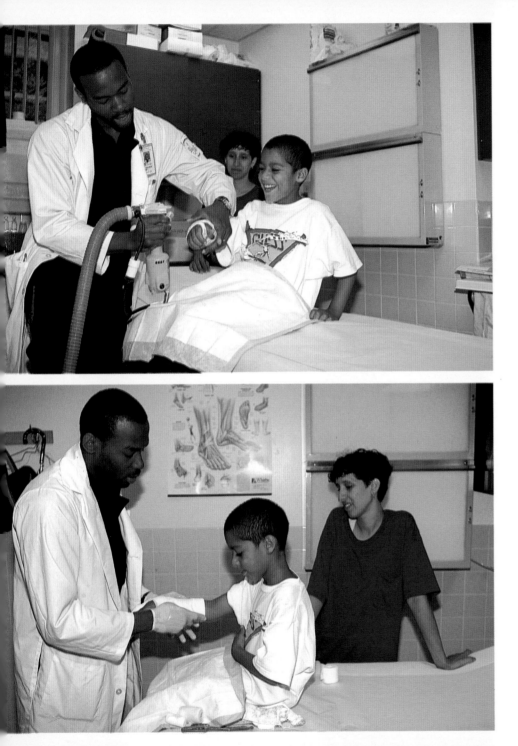

It's not too serious, but I need a permanent cast. A male nurse will take care of that. First he has to cut off the temporary one with a handsaw! Then he puts a white sock soaked in plaster of paris on my arm. When it dries, I can't even wiggle my wrist or arm. Finally he wraps a layer of red fiberglass over the cast and tells me not to get any water on this arm for *six weeks*. And all I can think is, now I can't go to the big swimming pool near the center. Mom gets mad when I use bad words. Sometimes it's hard *not* to.

Anyway, I'm sure not going to let this cast spoil my fun. I like to play with my little brother and sisters. I think Destiny kind of looks up to me as her big brother. But once in a while, she tells Mom that I boss her too much. Then she teases me, and that's when we fight.

I've made a lot of new friends since we came here. One of them is Shaheen. We meet in front of the building and walk over to a playground. We start playing basketball with a bunch of kids and I'm having a great time. The next thing I know, three tough-looking guys are standing around me. One of them sticks his fist in my face and yells, "Beat it, squirt! We don't want no homeless creeps playin' around here!" I may be small, but I'm real fast. Before he can land a punch, I'm gone—they'll never catch me. Three against one are dumb odds.

"Aw, the hell with them, Mikey," Shaheen says, catching up. "Let's see what's happening at the school yard." A few older kids are playing dodgeball and ask us to join in. This is a whole lot better.

Dinner tonight is spaghetti and meat sauce. I fix myself a spaghetti sandwich. I can see Destiny watching me. It must look good to her because she starts to make one for herself.

After watching TV for a while, I decide I've had enough. I don't like other people to see me when I'm feeling down. Sometimes, like now, when I'm hurting real bad, I have to shut myself in my room so nobody will see me cry. Sometimes I wonder if I'll *ever* have a home of my own. What scares me the worst is maybe one day we'll all wind up living on the city streets.

Destiny comes in and says it's time to go to bed. She shares my bunk with me now because she's afraid to sleep by herself. She's having bad dreams.

Yesterday my cast *finally* came off. Today is Labor Day. It's my last chance to get to the swimming pool. An older friend grabs me under the arms and tosses me high in the air. This is great! "Do it again," I beg. This is the best fun I've had all summer. Next week I've got to go back to school–*again*.

To tell the truth, fourth grade isn't as bad as I thought it would be. My new teacher, Miss Lucchese, is strict but fair. By the time winter comes, I have to admit I'm starting to like it. Well, a *little*, anyway.

When my mother was in high school, she had to leave before graduating. She was expecting her first baby: me, Mikey. This morning she's taking a G.E.D. exam downstairs in the office. If she does good, she'll get her high school diploma. She wants to go back to school and study to become a nurse's aide, but first she needs that diploma.

Alberto Gonzalez, the educational guidance counselor, studies her test papers. Then he shows her the mistakes she's made. Mom thinks she's flunked, but she's wrong. She's passed with top marks!

It'll be Christmas soon. Nothing's changed for my family. There's still no apartment for us to move to. But we haven't had a real Christmas together for three years. This time Mom says she's going to change that, no matter what happens.

Every year the Henry Street Settlement throws a big Christmas party for all the kids who live at the center. I love parties. There's carol singing and dancing, whipped cream cake and fruit punch. But for us kids, the main event is when our caseworkers hand out Christmas gifts.

We're all holding our breath while Jerry Purnell yells the name on each wrapped package. I'm hoping for a basketball. When my name is called, I look into a big bag and poke through the wrapping. Guess what? You're right!

Mom's bought a small tree and decorated it. She's also bought gifts for all of us. On Christmas morning, we wake her up at six o'clock, begging to see what Santa has brought. There's a big doll with a doctor kit for Destiny, a basketball game and a toy car for Sergio Jr., a doll for baby Laura, and a terrific video game for me!

I know how hard it was for Mom to pay for all these gifts. When I'm older, I want to go to college. When I start working, I want to help my mother have a better life. Most of all, when I grow up, I want to *be* somebody, somebody who really matters.